FEROCIOUS FIGHTING ANIMALS

HONEY BADGERS

Julia J. Quinlan

PowerKiDS press

New York

Published in 2013 by The Rosen Publishing Group, Inc.
29 East 21st Street, New York, NY 10010

First Edition

Editor: Amelie von Zumbusch
Book Design: Andrew Povolny

Photo Credits: Cover, pp. 10–11 HPH Image Library/Gallo Images/Getty Images; pp. 4–5 Ewan Chesser/Shutterstock.com; pp. 6, 20–21 Doug Cheeseman/Peter Arnold/Getty Images; p. 7 Mary Ann McDonald/Visuals Unlimited/Getty Images; p. 8 David Tipling/Oxford Scientific/Getty Images; p. 9 Whittaker Terry/Photo Researchers/Getty Images; pp. 12–13 Emil Von Maltitz/Oxford Scientific/Getty Images; pp. 12, 16 Christian Heinrich/Getty Images; p. 13 Martin Harvey/Digital Vision/Getty Images; p. 14 Michal Cizek/AFP/Getty Images; p. 15 © NHPA/Superstock; p. 17 (top) clickit/Shutterstock.com; p. 17 (bottom) Tobias Bernhard/Photolibrary/Getty Images; p. 18 Anup Shah/Photodisc/Thinkstock; p. 19 © Corbis/SuperStock; p. 22 © Abpl Library/Animals Animals.

Library of Congress Cataloging-in-Publication Data

Quinlan, Julia J.
  Honey badgers / by Julia J. Quinlan. — 1st ed.
     p. cm. — (Ferocious fighting animals)
Includes index.
ISBN 978-1-4488-9671-4 (library binding) — ISBN 978-1-4488-9800-8 (pbk.) —
ISBN 978-1-4488-9801-5 (6-pack)
1. Honey badger—Juvenile literature. I. Title.
QL737.C25Q45 2013
599.76'62—dc23
                                            2012026344

Manufactured in the United States of America

CPSIA Compliance Information: Batch #W13PK5: For Further Information contact Rosen Publishing, New York, New York at 1-800-237-9932

CONTENTS

MEET THE HONEY BADGER!   4

HONEY BADGER HABITATS   6

SKUNK LOOK-ALIKES   8

NIGHTTIME HUNTERS   10

FEROCIOUS HONEY BADGERS   12

BABY HONEY BADGERS   14

WHAT DO THEY EAT?   16

HONEY BADGER PREDATORS   18

PEOPLE AND HONEY BADGERS   20

TOUGH HONEY BADGERS   22

GLOSSARY   23

INDEX   24

WEBSITES   24

MEET THE HONEY BADGER!

The honey badger is one of the toughest animals on Earth. Honey badgers might not look that scary at first glance, but they are actually vicious fighters! They are called honey badgers because they like to eat honey. They are also known as ratels. Honey badgers are related to weasels and otters. However, they are much more ferocious than their relatives!

Honey badgers have claws they use for fighting and digging. They have sharp teeth. One of the most amazing things about honey badgers is their **resistance** to snake **venom**. Snakebites that would kill other animals only put the honey badger to sleep for a little while!

Some people consider honey badgers to be the world's most fearless animals.

HONEY BADGER HABITATS

Honey badgers are found in many places. They live in the Middle East, India, parts of central Asia, and most of Africa. These areas cover many **habitats**. The honey badger can live in **arid** habitats, or kinds of land that are quite dry. It is also found in rain forests and many habitats in between.

Some honey badgers, such as these, live on savannas. Savannas are flat grasslands with some trees.

Honey badgers like to live in underground homes called burrows. They use their claws to dig burrows for themselves. Sometimes honey badgers will move into burrows dug by other animals, such as aardvarks. Honey badgers will live in tree trunks or in caves if they cannot make or find burrows.

This honey badger is peering out of its burrow. The burrows that honey badgers dig themselves tend to be about 3 to 10 feet (1–3 m) long.

SKUNK LOOK-ALIKES

Honey badgers have black hair covering most of their bodies. They have white stripes that go down their backs, from the tops of their heads to their tails. They have similar coloring to skunks.

Honey badgers use their long claws to reach into crevices to catch bugs and other small animals to eat.

Like skunks, they also have body parts that make them smell really bad! The smell helps drive predators away.

Honey badgers are usually about 2 to 2.5 feet (61–76 cm) long and 8 to 12 inches (20–30 cm) tall. They have strong legs and long claws. Honey badgers have loose skin that lets them twist around to get away from predators or to attack them.

Honey badgers can climb trees. They do so to reach foods, such as bird eggs, snakes, and beehives.

NIGHTTIME HUNTERS

Honey badgers are not friendly animals. For the most part, they live alone. Honey badgers are **nocturnal**. That means they are most active at night. Honey badgers will sometimes be awake at dusk and dawn but are rarely up during daylight.

Honey badgers have **home ranges**, or areas in which they live. The home range of a male honey badger can be up to 200 square miles (518 sq km). Females have smaller ranges of about 50 square miles (130 sq km). Honey badgers move around a lot. They do not stay in the same burrow for long. This lets them avoid predators and find more food.

Honey badgers leave scent markings around their home ranges to let other honey badgers know that they are living there.

NIGHTTIME HUNTERS

Honey badgers are not friendly animals. For the most part, they live alone. Honey badgers are **nocturnal**. That means they are most active at night. Honey badgers will sometimes be awake at dusk and dawn but are rarely up during daylight.

Honey badgers have **home ranges**, or areas in which they live. The home range of a male honey badger can be up to 200 square miles (518 sq km). Females have smaller ranges of about 50 square miles (130 sq km). Honey badgers move around a lot. They do not stay in the same burrow for long. This lets them avoid predators and find more food.

Honey badgers leave scent markings around their home ranges to let other honey badgers know that they are living there.

Like skunks, they also have body parts that make them smell really bad! The smell helps drive predators away.

Honey badgers are usually about 2 to 2.5 feet (61–76 cm) long and 8 to 12 inches (20–30 cm) tall. They have strong legs and long claws. Honey badgers have loose skin that lets them twist around to get away from predators or to attack them.

Honey badgers can climb trees. They do so to reach foods, such as bird eggs, snakes, and beehives.

SKUNK LOOK-ALIKES

Honey badgers have black hair covering most of their bodies. They have white stripes that go down their backs, from the tops of their heads to their tails. They have similar coloring to skunks.

Honey badgers use their long claws to reach into crevices to catch bugs and other small animals to eat.

Honey badgers like to live in underground homes called burrows. They use their claws to dig burrows for themselves. Sometimes honey badgers will move into burrows dug by other animals, such as aardvarks. Honey badgers will live in tree trunks or in caves if they cannot make or find burrows.

This honey badger is peering out of its burrow. The burrows that honey badgers dig themselves tend to be about 3 to 10 feet (1–3 m) long.

FEROCIOUS
HONEY BADGERS

Honey badgers are fierce fighters. They will attack any animal that threatens them. They fight dangerous snakes, such as cobras, puff adders, vipers, and black mambas. Honey badgers are quick and never give up. They chase other animals up trees, underground, and into the bush.

BABY HONEY BADGERS

Honey badgers take a break from their **solitary** lifestyle when it is time to mate, or make babies. In many places, male and female honey badgers mate in September and October.

Female honey badgers generally give birth to one baby at a time but will sometimes have two.

This mother honey badger is caring for her baby. Young honey badgers tend to stay with their mothers for over one year.

Mother honey badgers carry their babies in their mouths. They move their babies from one den to another every few days.

Baby honey badgers are usually born in May. The babies are born without any hair. Their hair starts to grow after about two weeks. Male honey badgers do not stay with the mother and baby.

Honey badgers in **captivity** have lived as long as 26 years. Scientists are not sure how long honey badgers live in the wild.

WHAT DO THEY EAT?

Though honey badgers are named for their love of honey, they are **carnivores**. They eat mostly meat. Honey badgers eat just about anything they can catch! They eat snakes, birds, and insects. They also eat small **mammals** and the young of larger mammals.

Honey badgers often use their excellent sense of smell to find food.

When a honey badger finds a beehive, it doesn't just eat the honey inside. It also eats the bee **larvae**. Bees sting honey badgers that attack their hives. The badgers' thick skin keeps them from being too badly hurt, though.

Honey badgers eat young antelopes, such as this kudu calf.

Honey badgers sometimes follow birds called honey guides to find hives. After the badgers break the hives open, the birds feast on honey and larvae, too.

Many people consider the puff adder to be Africa's most dangerous snake. However, it is one of many snakes that honey badgers eat!

17

HONEY BADGER PREDATORS

Honey badgers may be tough and fearless, but that doesn't mean they do not have predators! Large mammals, such as lions and leopards, sometimes hunt honey badgers. Even honey badgers are no match for these big cats!

Like honey badgers, leopards live in both Asia and Africa.

Even though they are not that big, honey badgers are so tough that many predators just leave them alone.

Smaller animals try to prey on the honey badger, but the honey badger knows how to defend itself. Honey badgers fight back using their teeth and claws. Their thick skin protects them from many bites and its looseness allows them to wriggle away or reposition themselves to bite their attackers. Honey badgers can also spray attackers, just as skunks can.

PEOPLE AND HONEY BADGERS

Humans are the honey badger's most dangerous enemies. Many people who live in areas with honey badgers do not like them. That is because honey badgers often go onto farms at night and eat livestock or chickens. Many farmers will kill honey badgers if they see them.

Honey farmers especially dislike the honey badger. Honey badgers will destroy beehives, which leaves honey farmers with less honey to sell. Since honey badgers eat bee larvae, the farmers end up with fewer bees to make honey, too. Honey farmers set traps for honey badgers. They also poison them.

Though some people consider honey badgers pests, others admire their toughness.

TOUGH HONEY BADGERS

Even though honey badgers are hunted by people and get themselves into lots of dangerous fights, they are not **endangered**. It is hard to know exactly how many honey badgers there are because they are found in so many places and live alone most of the time.

Honey badgers can fight off most animals. They almost never back down from fights. They get stung by bees and bitten by snakes but keep eating. These incredibly tough animals are among the world's most ferocious fighters.

You wouldn't want to get into a fight with a honey badger!

GLOSSARY

arid (A-rud) Quite dry.

captivity (kap-TIH-vih-tee) A place where animals live, such as in a home, a zoo, or an aquarium, instead of living in the wild.

carnivores (KAHR-neh-vorz) Animals that eat mostly other animals.

endangered (in-DAYN-jerd) In danger of no longer existing.

habitats (HA-buh-tats) The kinds of land where animals or plants naturally live.

home ranges (HOHM RAYN-jez) Areas in which animals usually stay.

larvae (LAHR-vee) Animals in the early period of life in which they have a wormlike form.

mammals (MA-mulz) Warm-blooded animals that have backbones and hair, breathe air, and feed milk to their young.

nocturnal (nok-TUR-nul) Active during the night.

resistance (rih-ZIS-tens) A force that works against another force.

solitary (SAH-leh-ter-ee) Spending most time alone.

venom (VEH-num) A poison passed by one animal into another through a bite or a sting.

INDEX

B

burrow(s), 7, 10

C

caves, 7
claws, 4, 7, 9, 19

F

fighters, 4, 13, 22
fights, 22

H

home range(s), 10
homes, 7
honey, 4, 16–17, 20

I

India, 6

K

kinds, 6

L

land, 6
larvae, 17, 20

M

mammals, 16, 18
Middle East, 6

O

otters, 4

WEBSITES

Due to the changing nature of Internet links, PowerKids Press has developed an online list of websites related to the subject of this book. This site is updated regularly. Please use this link to access the list: www.powerkidslinks.com/ffa/badg/